BOMBING WITHOUT MOONLIGHT

Bakht-i jevan yar-i ma
dadan-i jan kar-i ma
qafile-salar-i ma
fakhr-e jehan Mustafast

—Mawlawi Rumi

BOMBING
WITHOUT
MOONLIGHT

THE ORIGINS OF SUICIDAL TERRORISM

Abdal Hakim Murad

Quilliam Press

First published 2008 by Amal Press
This edition 2022 by The Quilliam Press,
14 St Paul's Road, Cambridge CB1 2EZ

www.quilliampress.com

First published in *Encounters: Journal of Inter-Cultural Perspectives* 10 (2004), 85-118.

ISBN 978 1 872038 26 1

Cover design: Partners In Print / AAM

Printed in Turkey by Mega Print

CONTENTS

I

AMNESIA

TTENTION DEFICIT DISORDER seems to flourish under conditions of late modernity. The past becomes itself more quickly. Memories, individual as well as collective, tend to be recycled and consulted only by the old. For everyone else, there are only current affairs, reaching back a few months at most. Orwell, of course, predicted this, in his dystopic prophecy that may have been only premature; but today it seems to be cemented by postmodernism (Deleuze), and also by physicists, who are now proclaiming an almost Ash'arite scepticism about claims for the real duration of particles.

This is a condition that has an ancestry in the stirrings of the modernity which it represents. Hume anticipated it in his stunning insistence on the non-continuity of the human self: we are 'nothing but a collection of perceptions which succeed each other with inconceivable rapidity and are in perpetual flux and movement;' or so he thought.[1] Modern fiction may still explore or reaffirm identities (Peter Carey) and thus define human dignity as the honourable disposition of at least some aspects of an accumulated heritage. But this is giving way to the atomistic, playful, postmodern storytelling of, say, Elliot Perlman, which defines dignity – where it does so at all – in terms of *freedom* from all stories, even while lamenting the superficial tenor of the result. It is against the backdrop of this culture that the scientists, now far beyond Ataturk's 'Science is the Truest Guide in Life', raise the stakes with their occasionalism, and, for the neurologists, the increasing denial of the autonomy of the human will – a new predestinarianism that makes us always the consequence of genes and the present, not the remembered past.[2]

Our public conversations, then, seem to be the children of a marriage of convenience between two principles, neither of them religious or even particularly humanistic. The elitist mystical trope of the moment being all that is, significantly misappropriated by some New Age discourses, has become the condition of us all, albeit with the absence of God. Journalism thus becomes the privileged discourse to whose canons the public intellectual must conform, if he or she is to become a credible guide. More striking still is the observed fact that amidst our current crisis of wisdom it also seems to provide the language in which the public discussion of faith is carried on. Thus Catholicism becomes the humiliated cardinal of Boston, not St Augustine. Its morality is taken to be that which visibly clashes with the caprice of characters in *Home and Away*, not a severe but ultimately liberating cultivation of the virtues rooted in centuries of experience and example. Judaism, in its turn, becomes the latest land-grab of a settler rabbi, not a millennial enterprise of faith and promise. Of course, our new occasionalism does invoke the past. But it does so with reference either to scriptures, stripped of their normative exegetical armature, or to those events which remain in the consciousness of a citizenry raised on enlightenment battles with obscurantism. So again, we recall Galileo, not Eckhart; we recall the interesting hatreds of the Inquisition, not the charity of St Vincent de Paul. Otherwise, our culture is religiously amnesiac. Winston Churchill, near the end of his life, began to read the Bible. 'This book is very well-written,' he said. 'Why was it not brought to my attention before?'

It is in this frankly primitive condition that we seek to discuss religious acts which, against all the predictions of our grandparents, claim to interrupt the progress of history towards a world in which there will be no continuity at all. To our perplexity, history, despite Fukuyama, does not seem to have ended. Humans do not always act for the economic or erotic now; Tamino still seeks his Sarastro. A residue of real human diversity persists. For the human soul is not yet, as Meredith wrote,

> Seraphically free,
> From taint of personality.[3]

This failed ultimacy, this sense that we, the Papageni, have to dust down the armour of an earlier generation of moral absolutes, when history was still running, when the victory of the corporations and of Hollywood was not yet assured, accounts for the maladroit condition of the world's current argument about terrorism. The most active in seizing the moment, as they elbow impatiently past the *fin de siécle* multiculturalists and postmodernists, are the oddly-named American neoconservatives, who invoke Leo Strauss and roll up their sleeves to defend Washington against Oriental warriors who would defy the dialectics of history and seek to postpone the apotheosis of Anglo-Saxon consumer society, which they see as the climax of a billion years of evolution.[4] But despite such ideologised adversions to the *longue durée*, secularism seems to have little to offer that is not short-termist and reactive, and determined to reduce the globe to a set of variations on itself.

Traditionalists, who should be more helpful, seem paralysed. Much of the fury and hurt that currently abounds in the Christian and the Muslim worlds reveals a sense that the timetable which God has approved for history has been perverted. Christendom is not a virgin in this respect; in fact, it was first, with scholastic and Byzantine broadsides against Christian sin as invitation to Saracenic chastisement (Bernard, Gregory Palamas). Then it was the turn of Islam, when, from the seventeenth century on the illusion of the Muslims as materially and militarily God's chosen people was dealt a series of shocking blows. Now it is, once again, the turn of Christendom (if the term be still allowed), which is currently wondering why history has not yet experienced closure, why a former rival should still be showing signs of life, either as the result of a misdiagnosis, or as a zombie-like revenant bearing only a superficial resemblance to his medieval seriousness. Certainly, the American president and his frequently evangelical team see themselves in these terms. Architects of a society which, Disney-like, appropriates the past only to emphasise the glory of the present, these zealots appeal to a prophecy-religion in which the Book of Revelation is the key to history. For them, too, the promised closure is imminent, and its frustration by the Other an outrage.

President Reagan, while less captivated by end-time visions than his successors, could offer these thoughts to Jewish lobbyists:

> You know, I turn back to your ancient prophets in the Old Testament and the signs foretelling Armageddon and I find myself wondering if we're the generation that is going to see that come about. I don't know if you've noted any of these prophecies lately, but, believe me, they certainly describe the times we're going through.[5]

The protagonists of the current conflict, then, are unusual in their confidence that history has not ended, although millennialism seems to hover in the background on both sides, helped along by the frequently Palestinian scenery. The triumph of the West, or the resurgence of an Islam interpreted by bestselling Pentecostal authors as a chastisement and a demonic challenge, signals the end of a growing worry about the religious meaninglessness of late modernity. Tragically, however, neither protagonist seems validly linked to the remnants of established religion, or shows any sign of awareness of how to connect with history. Fundamentalist disjuncture is placing us in a kind of meta-historical parenthesis, an end-time excitement in which, as for St Paul, old rules are irrelevant, and Christ and Antichrist are the only significant gladiators on the stage. Fundamentalists, as well as mystics, can insist that the moment is all that is real.

II

SUNNA CONTRA

GENTILES

IN SUCH A world of pseudo-religious reaction against the postmodern erosion of identity, it follows that if you are not 'with us,' you are with the devil. Or, when this has to be reformulated for the benefit of the blue-collar godless, you are a 'cheese-eating surrender monkey'. Where religion exists to supply an identity, the world is Augustinian, if not quite Manichean. The West's ancient trope of itself as a free space, perhaps a white space, holding out against Persian or Semitic intruders, is being coupled powerfully, but hardly for the first time, with Pauline and patristic understandings of the New Israel as unique vessel of truth and salvation, threatened in the discharge of its redemptive project by the Oriental, Semitic, Ishmaelitic other. In the West, at least, the religious resources for this dualism are abundant and easily abused. Take Daniel Goldhagen, for instance, who in his most recent book suggests that the xenophobia of the Christian Bible is qualitatively *greater* than that of any other scripture. New Bibles, he urges, must be printed with many corrections to what he describes as this founding text of a lethal Western self-centredness.[1] Semites of several kinds would be well-advised to beware a culture raised on such a foundation.

It is remarkable that both sides, in constructing themselves against a wicked, fundamentalist rival, mobilise the ancient trope of antisemitism. The Self needs its dark Other, preferably nearby or within. That Other has standard features: in the case of Christian antisemitism it is that it stands for Letter rather than Spirit, for blind obedience rather than freedom, for an discreet but intense transnational solidarity in place of Fatherland and Church. It is sexually aberrant (hence the Nazi polemic against Freud). It hides its women (who should, instead, join the SS, or practice *nacktkultur*). It imposes archaic and unscientific taboos: diet, purity, circumcision. Such are the categories in which an almost dualistic West historically defines its relationship to its nearest and most irritating Other.[2]

Antisemitism is, in Richard Harries' words, a 'light sleeper'. But part of its strength is that it is not asleep at all; and never has been. As Christendom seeks its identity, the Dark Other today is now more usually Ishmael. Torched mosques, terrified asylum-seekers, bullied schoolchildren, and, we may not unreasonably add, a journalistic discourse of the type that is now being labelled 'Islamophobic', are less new than they seem. They represent a *vicarious* antisemitism. 'Islamic law is immutable' is a chorus in the new Horst Wessel song. 'Circumcision is barbaric.' 'Their divorce laws are medieval and anti-woman.' 'They keep to themselves and don't integrate.' Such is the battle-cry of the resurgent Western right: Pim Fortuin, Jean-Marie Le Pen, Jorg Haider, Filip de Winter. It has become startlingly popular, though always volatile at the polls. Thus is the old anti-semitic metabolism of Europe and its American progeny being reinvigorated by the encounter with Ishmael. Again, history has started up again, and again our amnesiac culture ignores the vast cogwheels, deep beneath the surface, which move it.

On the other side, now, crossing the Mediterranean, or the Timor Sea, we generally find not a bloc of sincere fundamentalist regimes, but an archipelago of dictatorships, Oriental despots after the letter, which are in almost every case answerable not to their own electorates – for they recognise none – but to a distant desk in the State Department.³ These are the neo-mamluks, ex-soldiers and condottieri of a system that penalises ethics. Ranged against them we observe the puritans, iconoclasts with El Greco eyes, whose claim it is to detest the modernity of the regimes. Such puritans, led by the memory of Sayyid Qutb, have no illusions about the nature of secular rule. They see clearly that the regimes are *more* modern than those of the West, because more frank in their conviction that science plus commerce does not equal ethics. Where the Western journalistic eye sees retardation, the Islamist sees modernity. Hitler and Stalin were more modern than Churchill and Roosevelt, more scientific, more programmatic, more distant from the past. The future is theirs, and it is neither Christ's millennial reign nor the triumph of small-town America. It is Alphaville.

The Islamist, then, is not the caricature of the envious, uncomprehending Third Worlder. Typically he has spent much of his life in the West, and is capable of offering an empirical analysis, or at least a diagnosis. Sayyid Qutb, in his writing on what he calls 'the deformed birth of the American man,' sees Americans as advanced infants; advanced because of their technology, but puerile in their ignorance of earlier stages of human development.⁴ There is something of Teilhard de Chardin in his account, which inverts Tocqueville to identify an American idiot-savant mania for possession. Technology made America possible, and ultimately, America need claim nothing else. Linked to Christian fundamentalism, it is an enemy of every other story; and unlike the East, it will not remain in its place. It must send out General Custer to subdue all remnants of earlier phases of human consciousness rooted in nature, spirituality or art. Its client regimes are therefore its natural, not opportunistic, adjuncts in its programme to subdue the world. They are not a transitional phase, they are the end-game.

Antisemitism forms part of this vision too, certainly. But since, as Goldhagen confirms, this is an essentially Christian phenomenon, to be healed by correcting the views of the Evangelists, in an Islamic context which lacks a letter-spirit dichotomy it seems a hazier resource for identity construction. Qutb was influenced by the Vichy theorist Alexis Carrel (1873–1944), through his odd, vitalist tract L'Homme, cet inconnu, which remains an ultimate, though unacknowledged, source text for much modern Islamism.[5] No medieval Muslim thinker of any note wrote a book against Judaism, although homilies against Christianity were quite common. If medieval Islam had a dark Other, it was more likely to be Zoroastrianism than Judaism, which, in Samuel Goitein's phrase by which he summed up his magisterial work A Mediterranean Society, enjoyed a close and 'symbiotic' relationship with Islam.[6] But today's Qutbian Islamist purges midrashic material from Koranic commentary, and studies the Tsarist forgery The Protocols of the Learned Elders of Zion, and, even, Mein Kampf. Nothing can be discovered, it seems, in the Islamic libraries, so that this importation into an ostensively nativist and xenophobic milieu becomes inescapable – the fundamentalist's familiar appeal to necessity.

As he surveys the wreckage of Istanbul synagogues and Masonic lodges, the journalist, as ibn al-waqt, is oblivious to the happier past of Semitic conviviality in the Ottoman Sephardic lands. And perhaps he is right, perhaps, under our conditions, the past is another religion. But the paradox has become so burning, and so murderous, that we cannot let it pass unremarked. The Islamic world, instructed to host Israel, was historically the least inhospitable site for the diaspora. The currently almost ubiquitous myth of a desperate sibling rivalry between Isaac and Ishmael is nonsensical to historians.

Here, at the dark heart of Islam's extremist fringe, we find what may be the beginnings of a solution. No nativist reaction can long survive proof of its own exogenous nature. And no less than its Christian analogues, Islamic ghuluww, at least in its currently terroristic forms, betrays a European etiology. It borrows its spiritual, as well as its material, armament from Western modernity. This, we may guess, marks it out for anachronism in a context where intransigence is xenophobic.[7]

This is an unpopular diagnosis; but one which is gaining ground. It cannot be without significance that outside observers, when not blinded by a xenophobic need to view terrorism as Islamically authentic, have sometimes intuited this well. Here, for instance, is the verdict of John Gray, in his book *Al-Qaeda and What it Means to be Modern*:

> No cliche is more stupefying than that which describes Al-Qaida as a throwback to medieval times. It is a by-product of globalisation. Its most distinctive feature—projecting a privatised form of organised violence worldwide—was impossible in the past. Equally, the belief that a new world can be hastened by spectacular acts of destruction is nowhere found in medieval times. Al-Qaida's closest precursors are the revolutionary anarchists of late nineteenth-century Europe.[8]

And Slavoj Zizek, a still more significant observer, is convinced that what we are witnessing is not 'Jihad versus MacWorld'—the standard leftist formulation—but rather MacWorld versus MacJihad.[9]

This implies that if *ghuluww* has a future, it will be because modernity has a future, not because it has roots in Islamic tradition. That tradition, indeed, it rules out of order, as it dismisses the juridical, theological and mystical intricacies of medieval Islam as so much dead wood. The solution, then, which the world is seeking, and which it is the primary responsibility of the Islamic world, not the West to provide, must be a counter-reformation, driven by our best and most cosmopolitan heritage of spirit and law.

A point of departure, here, and a useful retort to essentialist reductions of Islam to Islamism, is the fact that orthodoxy still flies the flag in almost all seminaries. The reformers are, at least institutionally, in the Rhonnda chapels, not the cathedrals. Perhaps the most striking fact about regulation Sunni Islam over the past fifty years has been its insistence that religion's general response to modernity must not take the form of an armed struggle. There have been local exceptions to this rule, as in the reactive wars against Serbian irredentism in Bosnia, and Soviet intrusion into Afghanistan. But a doctrine of generic *jihad* against the West has been conspicuous by its absence.[10]

It is not immediately clear how we gloss this. In the nineteenth century Sunni Islam frequently elected to resist European colonial rule by force, giving rise to the figure of the Mad Mullah who formed part of the imperial imagination, in the fiction of John Buchan, or Tolstoy's *Hajji Murad*. In the twentieth century, however, the traditional pragmatism of Sunnism seemed to generate an ulema ethos that was certainly not quietist, but had nothing in common with Qutbian Islamism either. Hence the Deobandi movement in India, and its Tablighi offshoot, supported the Congress party, and generally opposed Partition. Arab religious leaders sometimes resorted to force, as with the Naqshbandi shaykh Izz al-Din al-Qassam in mandate Palestine; but the independence movements were overwhelmingly directed by secular modernists. The ancient universities, al-Qarawiyyin, al-Zaytuna, al-Azhar and the rest, regarded the modern period as a mandate for doctrinal retrenchment and the piecemeal *ijtihad*-based reassessment of aspects of Islamic law. In other words, mainstream Islam's response to the startling novelty of a modernity that was forced on its societies at the point of an imperial or postcolonial bayonet was self-scrutinising and cautious, not militant.

Traditional wisdom and the texts, of course, were the reason for this. Sunnism, as inscribed by the great Seljuk theorists, had put its trust in prudence, pragmatism, and a strategy of negotiation with the sultan. So in British India, the Hanafi consensus decided that the Raj formed part of *dar al-islam*. In Russia, Shihab al-Din Marjani took the same view with regard the empire of the Tsars. But for Qutb, all this was paradigmatic of the error of classical Sunni thought. Islam was to be prophetic, and hence a liberation theology, challenging structures as well as souls, not by preaching and praying alone, but by agitation and revolution. Given his education and *sitz im leben* in the golden age of anti-colonialism, probably nothing could have extricated Qutb from his critique of what he saw as Sunni indifferentism, rooted, he suspected, in Ash'ari deontology and a presumed Sufi fatalism. The prophetic is not *meant* to be accommodating; it fails, or it succeeds triumphantly. The normative political thinkers, Mawardi, Nizam al-Mulk, Ghazali, Katib Çelebi, and their modern advocates, had to be jettisoned. Technological empires had made the world anew, and, if it was to cope with an increasingly bizarre and offensive Other, Islamic thought had to be reformed in the direction of an increasingly unconditional insurrectionism.

Qutb's resurrection of Ibn Taymiya, via Rashid Rida, became paradigmatic. In the fourteenth century this angry Damascene had attacked ulema who acquiesced in the rule of the nominally Muslim Mongols. Loyalty could be to a righteous imam alone. Rida and others had taken pains to dissociate this from the Kharijite slogan 'No rule other than God's', for an unpleasant odour hung about the name of Kharijism. But *de facto*, the hard wing of Hanbalite Islam seemed vulnerable to a Kharijite reading. Prototypical al-Qaida supporters wrote to condemn the Syrian neo-Hanbali scholar Nasir al-Din al-Albani, when he released a series of taped sermons entitled *Min Manhaj al-Khawarij*, 'From the Method of the Kharijites', in the early 1990s.[11] Often the word used by less radical puritans in Saudi Arabia for those engaged in terrorism is, precisely, 'Kharijite'.

What everyone agrees, however, is that al-Qaida is far, far removed from medieval Sunnism. For some, it is Kharijite; for others, an illicit Westernisation of Islam. As Carl Brown puts it, 'it cannot be stressed too often just how much Qutb's hardline interpretation departs from the main current of Islamic political thought throughout the centuries.'[12] For Brown, Qutbism is kharijism *redux*; but we would add, with Gray, that it is a Westernised kharijism. Like all identity movements, it ends with only a very arguable kind of authenticity.

The convergence between a malfunctioning Hanbalism and modern revolutionary vanguardism may owe its strength not to a shared potential for an instantiated xenophobia, although this will attract many party cadres; instead, I suspect, it relates to deeper structures of relationality with the world and its worldliness. The new Islamic zealotry is angry with the Islamic past, as Ibn Taymiya was. For Ibn Taymiya, the ulema had not adequately polarised light and dark. In the case of the mystics, they had disastrously confused them. There is something of the Augustine in Ibn Taymiya: a concrete understanding of a God who is radically apart from creation, or, in patristic terms, alienated from it, and a consequently high view of scripture that challenges Ash'arite and Maturidi confidences in the direct intelligibility of God in the world, and revives essentially dualistic readings of the Fall narrative. It may be that Ibn Taymiya's roots in Harran, scene of neo-Gnostic and astral speculations, parallel Augustine's Manichean background. But there is certainly a furious, single-minded zeal in both men that expresses itself in a deep pessimism about the human mind and conscience, and hence the worth of intellectuals, poets, logicians, and mystics.[13] In such a cosmology, which deploys the absolute polarity abhorred by Deleuze's *Pli* (his love of nomadic arts, with their 'blocs of sensations' is Islamically suggestive) gentilizing becomes first, not second nature.

Seljuk accommodationism, by contrast, had been driven by an ultimately Ghazalian moralism that feared the spiritual entailments of this crypto-dualism. Nizam al-Mulk, paradigm of high Sunni realpolitik, does not enforce a norm, but enforces the toleration of many norms. He finds that like all scripture, the Koran is super-replete, overflowing with meaning, and no exegete may taste all its flavours; this destabilising miracle may express itself in schism, historically the less favoured Islamic option, or in *adab al-ikhtilaf*, the forced courtesy of the scholar-jurist well aware of the ultimately unfixable quality of much of holy writ. The Sunni achievement, which was a moral as well as a pragmatic achievement, was to incorporate a wide spectrum of theological and juristic dispute into the universe of allowable internal difference. For zealotry, as Ghazali puts it, is a *hijab*, a veil.[14] It is a form of, in the Rabbis' language, loving the Torah more than God. A besetting *odium theologicum* which can only be healed through self-scrutiny and a due humility before the often baffling intricacy of God's word and world.

It was on the basis of this hospitable caution that non-Qutbian Sunnism engaged with modernity. Reading the fatwas of great twentieth-century jurists such as Yusuf al-Dajawi, Abd al-Halim Mahmud, and Subhi Mahmassani, one is reminded of the Arabic proverb cited on motorway signs in Saudi Arabia: *fi'l-ta'anni as-salama* - there is safety in reducing speed. Far from committing a pacifist betrayal, the normative Sunni institutions were behaving in an entirely classical way. Sunni piety appears as conciliatory, cautious, and disciplined, seeking to identify the positive as well as the negative features of the new global culture. Thus it is not the orthodox, but the merchants of identity religion, the *Sunna Contra Gentiles*, who insist on totalitarian and exclusionary readings of the Law and the state.[15]

If this is our curious situation, if al-Qaida is indeed a product and mirror not of the Sunni story, but of the worst of the Enlightenment's possibilities, if it is, as it were, the Frankenstein of Frankistan (as Zionism is a *golem*), how effective can be America's currently chosen antidote? This takes the form of killing, imprisoning and torturing the leadership, and many of the rank and file, using the methods which have been reported by British and other detainees released from Guantanamo Bay, and by Red Cross officials disturbed by news from Bagram air base in Kabul. Again, our occasionalism has allowed us to forget the history of revolutionary movements, which suggests that such measures are self-defeating, sowing the dragon's teeth of martyrdom, and announcing to the world the depth of the torturer's fear. A civilisation confident of victory would not resort to such desperate means. For after violence and internment, there is no last resort. Both moral advantage and deterrent threat have already been used up.

Traditional Sunnis intuit that al-Qaida is a Western invention, but one which cannot be defeated in a battleground where the logic is Western. This was one of the messages that emerged from the 2003 summit meeting of eight hundred Muslim scholars at Putrajaya.[16] Al-Qaida is inauthentic: it rejects the classical canons of Islamic law and theology, and issues fatwas that are neither formally nor in their habit of mind deducible from medieval exegesis. But it is not enough for the entire leadership of the religion to denounce al-Qaida, as it did at Putrajaya, and then to hope and pray that the same strange logic of modernity that bred this insurgency can spirit it away again. The West inseminates, but does not so easily abort. Faced with this, the Sunni leadership needs to be more alert to its responsibilities. Even the radical Westernisation of Islamic piety remains the responsibility of Muslim ulema, not, ultimately, of the Western matrix that inspired it. And it has to be said that the Sunni leadership has not done enough. Denunciations alone will not dent the puritan's armour, and may strengthen it; this the Counter-Reformation learned by experience.

III

JUS IN BELLO

THE WAR AGAINST neo-Kharijite ideology can only be won by Sunni normalcy. Washington's rhetoric of 'religion-building' disguises either a Texan missionary instinct or the triumphant relativism of the secular academy. Franklin Graham and the Ashcroft Inquisition will fail, as Christianity always does against Semitic monotheism, while liberalism, at once its rival and its hypocritical bedfellow, cannot be relied on to supply ethics under conditions of stress. For the Occidental energy all too often responds to such conditions either by apathy (remember the wartime Parisian intelligentsia), or by suspending the ethical teleologically, the classic revolutionary gambit since the days of the Paris commune, if not the English civil war.

The zealots of both sides insist that the validating of 'soft targets' is a representative Islamic act. How might they respond to evidence that it is, in fact, a representative secular-Western one? The evidence, as it turns out, is compelling, being a matter of historical record. Despite its claims in times of obese complacency to abhor the killing of the innocent, the secular West reverts with indecent haste to Cicero's maxim, *Silent enim leges inter arma* – laws are silent during war. And it is in this Occidental culture, and not in mainline Islam, that we should seek the matrix of radical Islamism. Let us survey the record.

W.G. Sebald has been a recent and helpful contributor here. He writes lyrically of the vengeance visited by the RAF on Germany's cities in the early 1940s, focussing on the thirty thousand who died in Operation Gomorrah (!) against the city of Hamburg. The object of such campaigns was military only in a very indirect way, for Churchill's purpose in what he called 'terror bombing' (where it was not straightforward vengefulness) was to sap the morale of Germany's civilian population. As Sebald shows, Parliament restructured the whole British economy to support the area bombing campaign, for one reason alone: it was the only way in which Britain could successfully strike back.[1]

In 1930, the British population had generally shared the view of one politician that to bomb civilians was 'revolting and un-English.'[2] But with its back against the wall, the population changed its mind with impressive speed. In 1942, Bomber Command's Directive No. 22 identified the 'morale of the enemy civil population' as the chief target. By the end of the war, a million tons of high explosive had rained down on German cities, and half a million civilians were dead. By that time a majority of Britons explicitly supported the bombing of civilian targets.[3] As the MP for Norwich put it: 'I am all for the bombing of working-class areas of German cities. I am Cromwellian – I believe in "slaying in the name of the Lord",'[4] while after Operation Gomorrah, a popular headline crowed that 'Hamburg has been Hamburgered.'[5] A third of the war economy was directed to serve this onslaught, with the development of new weapons of mass destruction, such as incendiary bombs, designed specifically to maximise devastation to private homes.[6] Yet after Dresden, which the postwar official history hailed as the 'crowning achievement' of the bombing campaign, Churchill was forced to reconsider:

> It seems to me that the moment has come when the question of bombing of German cities simply for the sake of increasing the

terror, though under other pretexts, should be reviewed.
Otherwise, we shall come into control of an utterly ruined land.[7]

This was no sort of repentance. To his last breath Churchill
defended the terror campaign which he had instigated and
which underpinned so much of his popularity. Mass destruction
from the air of a target whose details were often obscured by
clouds or the absence of moonlight, was not, for this icon of
English defiance, a moral problem.

A largely secular person of the stamp of our wartime Prime
Minister was clearly following a fairly standard Enlightenment
philosophy which had replaced the wars of kings with the wars of
peoples. Clausewitz, the chief architect of post-medieval military
thought, was certain that 'war is an act of force which theoreti-
cally can have no limits,'[8] a view that the most influential military
theorists of the twentieth century extended to the use of airpower
to terrorize civilians (Liddell Hart, Douhet, Harris). One might
have hoped that this illustration of the moral calibre of secularity
was found appalling by the Christian conscience of the day. But
the stance taken by the leaders of British Christianity was already
deeply influenced by modernism. The Archbishop of Canterbury
William Temple, followed by his brother bishop of York, consis-
tently refused to join the anti-terror minority within the Anglican
church. As a historian records, 'only a handful of the clergy
objected outright to area bombing;'[9] George Bell, the outspoken
Bishop of Chichester, was a lonely exception in upholding earlier
ideals of a just war which had regarded women and children as
sacrosanct.

After the war, the victors reset the moral template to its
rhetorical default position, and their earlier fatwas in favour of
terror bombing were relegated to an outer, uncomfortable edge
of the national memory. Once again, England and America
(which had carried on its own targeting of civilians in Japan)[10]
reverted to the traditional notion of civilian immunity, with its

pre-Enlightenment roots. So five years later, the British press felt able to excoriate Menachem Begin as a terrorist, simply because, as he puts it in his memoirs: 'our enemies called us terrorists [...] but we used physical force only because we were faced by physical force.'[11] And today, who can claim that Al-Qaida's logic is different? The 777 has become the poor man's nuclear weapon, his own Manhattan Project. Again, he has turned traitor to the East by embracing the utilitarian military ethic of his supposed adversary. He, even more than the regimes, shows the cost of Westernisation.

In this light, how may we take the pulse of the West's denunciation of 'Muslim terror'? Let us recall Adorno's First Law of sexual ethics: always mistrust the accuser.

IV

SAMSON TERRORISTES

THE TARGETING OF civilians is more Western than otherwise; contemplating the Ground Zero of a hundred German cities, this can hardly be denied. Yet it will be claimed that suicidal terrorism is something new, and definitively un-Western. Here, we are told by xenophobes on both sides, the Islamic suicide squads, the Black Widows, the death-dealing pilots, are an indigenously Islamic product.[1] And yet here again, when we detach ourselves from the emotive chauvinism of the Islamists and their Judeo-Christian misinterpreters, we soon find that the roots of such practices in the Islamic imagination are as recent as they are shallow. The genealogy of suicide bombing clearly stretches back from Palestine, through Shi'a guerillas in southern Lebanon, to the Hindu-nativist zealots of the Tamil Tigers, and to the holy warriors of Shinto Japan, who initiated the tradition of donning a bandanna and making a final testament on camera before climbing into the instrument of destruction. The kamikaze was literally the 'Wind of Heaven', a term evocative of the divine intervention which destroyed the Mongol fleet as it crossed the Yellow Sea.

Hindu and Buddhist tributaries of Middle-Eastern suicide bombing are conspicuous, and it is significant that the Islamists, driven as ever by nativist passion, recoil from them in fits of denial. (How happily, in the sermons, *hunud* rhymes with yahud!) Yet some scenic images may be instructive for those who take the philosophy of isnad seriously. After describing the Christian martyr Peregrinus, who set fire to himself in public, Sir James Frazier records:

> Buddhist monks in China sometimes seek to attain Nirvana by the same method, the flame of their religious zeal being fanned by a belief that the merit of their death redounds to the good of the whole community, while the praises which are showered upon them in their lives, and the prospect of the honours and worship which await them after death, serve as additional incentives to suicide.[2]

But it was in South India that holy suicide seems to have been most endemic:

> In Malabar and the neighbouring regions, many sacrifice themselves to the idols. When they are sick or involved in misfortune, they vow themselves to the idol in case they are delivered. Then, when they have recovered, they fatten themselves for one or two years; and when another festival comes around, they cover themselves with flowers, crown themselves with white garlands, and go singing and playing before the idol, when it is carried through the land. There, after they have shown off a good deal, they take a sword with two handles, like those used in currying leather, put it to the back of their necks, and cutting strongly with both hands sever their heads from their bodies before the idol.[3]

The atmaghataka, the suicidal Hindu, was a familiar sight of the premodern Indian landscape, where 'religious suicides were highly recommended and in most cases glorified.'[4] Suicide often functioned as the culmination of a pilgrimage: 'the enormous Tirtha literature (literature on pilgrimage) curiously enough describes in detail suicide by intending persons at different places of pilgrimage and the varying importance and virtues attached to them.'[5] Ibn Battuta and al-Biruni, among other Muslim visitors, had been particularly shocked by Hindu customs of sacred suicide, particularly bride-burning and self-drowning.[6] Altogether, in such a culture the development of suicidal methods as part of war is hardly surprising; they are deeply rooted in local non-monotheistic values.

Today's Tamil extremists extend this tradition in significant ways. Each Tamil Tiger wears a cyanide capsule around his neck, to be swallowed in case of capture. The explosive belt, used to assassinate hated politicians as well as Sinhalese marines and ordinary civilians, predates its Arab borrowing: the first Tamil suicide-martyrs in modern times appear in the 1970s.[7] The Tiger's Hindu roots[8] thus nourish the current Palestinian practice; as one observer notes: 'the Black Tigers, as the suicide cadres are known, have been emulated by the likes of Hamas.'[9]

But there is also a strong Western precedent, in pagan antiquity, in early Judaism, and in Christianity.

Suicide had been a respectable option for many ancients. Achilles chooses battle against the Trojans, knowing that the gods have promised that this will lead to his death. Ajax takes his own life, in the confidence that this will not affect his honour. Chrysippus, Zeno, and Socrates all opt for suicide rather than execution or dishonour. Marcus Aurelius praises it to the skies. It was only the neo-Platonists and late Platonists (who not coincidentally became the most congenial Hellenes for Islam) who systematically opposed it.[10]

The Biblical text nowhere condemns suicide. (Judas is condemned for betrayal, not for taking his own life; although Augustine will claim otherwise.) On the contrary, it offers several examples of individuals who chose death.[11] Saul (the koranic Talut) falls on his own sword rather than be humiliated in Philistine captivity (I Samuel 31). Jonah (Yunus) asks the frightened mariners to cast him into the sea (Jonah 1.12), and begs 'Take my life from me,' (4.3) for 'it is better for me to die than to live' (4.8–9). Job (Ayyub) prays: 'O that I might have my request, and that God would grant my desire; that it would please God to crush me' (Job 6:8–13), and even 'I loath my life' (7:15). Later, during the Maccabean revolts, the hero Razis falls on his sword to avoid falling into the hands of the wicked (2 Maccabees 14:42, 45–6). A notion of vicarious atonement has developed, so that the militant's suicide which enrages the enemy brings a blessing to the people (4 Maccabees 17:21–2).[12]

The early rabbis typically accept self-immolation in situations of military desperation, to avoid humiliation and to impress the enemy. The deaths of Saul and Samson were regarded as exemplary.[13] And in 'the Jewish Middle Ages, enthusiasm for martyrdom (at least in Ashkenaz - northern Europe) became so great that it proved a positive danger to Jewish existence.'[14] Religious voices raised in support of 20th century Zionism could link this tradition to their own militancy.[15] Hence Avram Kook, the first Ashkenazy Chief Rabbi of mandate Palestine (in Walter Wurzburger's words)

> permitted individuals to volunteer for suicide missions when carried out in the interest of the collective Jewish community. In other words, an act that would be illicit if performed to help individuals, would be legitimate if intended for the benefit of the community.[16]

In the nascent Christian movement, Jesus came to be presented as a suicide, albeit one who knew that he would be resurrected. Some historians are convinced that Jesus, having armed his band with swords (Luke 22:36), formed part of the larger Zealot movement against Roman oppression,[17] while others adhere to the orthodox view that his deliberate death was to be a cosmic sacrifice for human sin; but in either case, the dominant voice in the New Testament presents him as going to Jerusalem in the awareness that this would bring about his certain death (see Mark 10:32–4). Hence the insistent courting of martyrdom by many early Christians praised by Tertullian (here in the words of a modern scholar):

> In 185 the proconsul of Asia, Arrius Antoninus, was approached by a group of Christians demanding to be executed. The proconsul obliged some of them and then sent the rest away, saying that if they wanted to kill themselves there was plenty of rope available or cliffs they could jump off.[18]

And for Chrysostom, blasting the infidels, the Christians were better than the ancients, since Socrates had had little choice, while Christians volunteered for martyrdom. In fact, most orthodox Christian martyrs appear to have been volunteers, many of them appearing from nowhere to clamour for the death penalty, or emerging from the crowds to join the flames consuming one of their brethren. It was only with Augustine that this self-immolating behaviour came to an end, as involuntary martyrdom was established as the only acceptable Christian norm in the West.[19]

Orthodoxy, however, remained closer to the primitive tradition. As Frazier records (of sixteenth to nineteenth-century Russia): 'whole communities hailed with enthusiasm the gospel of death, and hastened to put its precepts into practice.' Although at first the volunteers were dropped into doorless rooms in which they starved to death 'for Christ', fire became the most popular method.

> Priests, monks, and laymen scoured the villages and hamlets preaching salvation by the flames, some of them decked in the spoils of their victims; for the motives of the preachers were often of the basest sort. They did not spare even the children,

but seduced them by promises of the gay clothes, the apples, the
nuts, the honey they would enjoy in heaven. [...] Men, women
and children rushed into the flames. Sometimes hundreds, and
even thousands, thus perished together.[20]

Combining the practice of suicidal martyrdom-seeking with the
pursuit of warfare, resulted, for Europeans as well as for Tamils,
in what would today be called suicidal warfare. This had the
advantage of generating tremendous publicity for the cause in
worlds such as the Indic and the Greco-Roman which, like today's,
had a penchant for the bizarre.[21] And for this, the most
spectacular precedent was in the Bible. Brian Wicker, a modern
Catholic interpreter, remarks that 'to us, Samson just appears
like a cross between Beowulf and Batman,'[22] while Bernhard
Anderson in his book *The Living World of the Old Testament*,
neutralises the Samson story by viewing him as the object of
divine punishment.[23] Yet he is presented by the narrator of Judges
13 to 16 as an unambiguous hero, and traditionally the churches
regarded his self-destruction and his massacre of three thousand
Philistine men, women, and children, as a valid act of martyrdom.
Augustine and Aquinas both pose the question: why is self-murder
not here a sin, and answer: because God had commanded him,
and the normal ethical rule was thus suspended.[24]

This suicide-warrior rises to the top of Western literature in
Samson Agonistes. Milton is here smarting from the horror and
shame of the Restoration. Once again, England is under the
idolatrous law of king and bishops, a kind of *jahiliyya*, and
Cromwell's city of glass has been shattered. His poem, then, is
autobiographical: Samson is a true hero, humiliated, blinded by
an unjust king, kept captive in the world of the dark Other. Like
the refugee-camp inmate he is

Exposed
To daily fraud, contempt, abuse and wrong,

> Within doors, or without, still as a fool,
> In power of others, never in my own.[25]

His duty, confronted by a hypocritical War on Terror, is to take effective revenge by any means necessary. His father, recognising this grim necessity, makes the usual statement of fathers of suicide bombers everywhere:

> Nothing is here for tears, nothing to wail,
> Or knock the breast, no weakness, no contempt,
> Dispraise, or blame, nothing but well and fair.
> And what may quiet us in a death so noble.[26]

The theme continues, through Handel, to reach Saint-Saens. In the latter's opera *Samson and Delilah* the Samson legend, far from falling by the wayside of progress and *fraternité*, seems the perfect icon for France's contemporary humiliation before Prussian technology. The guns of Krupp have frustrated France's destiny in her *mission civilatrice*, and the chosen people must be avenged. The story seems entirely modern: there is the theme of the tragic power of sex – Delilah becomes a second Carmen – and we witness the inevitability of total destruction in a grand, cast-iron *Götterdammerung*. Ernst Jünger, Stalingrad, and the suicidal B–52 captain in *Doctor Strangelove* are not far behind.

But perhaps the most recent, and also the most fascinating, mobilisation of the Samson 'ideal' in Western literature is the novel *Samson* by the Zionist ideologue Vladimir Jabotinsky. 'Homeland, whatever the price!' is the captured Israelite's slogan. Like the Islamist, the Zionist hero stresses the impossibility of conviviality:

> The second thing I have learned in the last few days is the
> wisdom of having boundary–stones [...] Neighbours can agree
> so long as each remains home, but trouble comes as soon as

they begin to pay each other visits. The gods have made men different and commanded them to respect the ditch in the fields. It is a sin for men to mix what the Gods have separated.[27]

Like a good Islamist, the Zionist Samson combines this xenophobia with a passion to acquire the Other's technology. When asked if he had a message for his own people, he cries:

They must get iron. They must give everything they have for iron – their silver and wheat, oil and wine and flocks, even their wives and daughters. All for iron! There is nothing in the world more valuable than iron. Will you tell them that?[28]

Like the Islamist, too, Jabotinsky's suicide-hero is envious of the unbeliever's skills at organisation:

One day, he was present at a festival at the temple of Gaza. Outside in the square a multitude of young men and girls were gathered for the festive dances [...] A beardless priest led the dances. He stood on the topmost step of the temple, holding an ivory baton in his hand. When the music began the vast concourse stood immobile [...] The beardless priest turned pale and seemed to submerge his eyes in those of the dancers, which were fixed responsively on his. He grew paler and paler; all the repressed fervor of the crowd seemed to concentrate within his breast till it threatened to choke him. Samson felt the blood stream to his heart; he himself would have choked if the suspense had lasted a few moments longer. Suddenly, with a rapid, almost inconspicuous movement, the priest raised his baton, and all the white figures in the square sank down on the left knee and threw the right arm towards heaven – a single movement, a single, abrupt, murmurous harmony. The tens of thousands of onlookers gave utterance to a moaning sigh. Samson staggered; there was blood on his lips, so tightly had he pressed them together [...] Samson left the place profoundly thoughtful. He could not have given words to his thought, but he had a feeling that here, in this spectacle of thousands obeying a single will, he had caught a glimpse of the great secret of politically minded peoples.[29]

Lest this be thought an aberrant, marginal use of the suicide-hero, let us recall the words of another Zionist thinker, Stephen Rosenfeld: 'All our generation was brought up on that book.'[30]

Samson provides an important Biblical archetype for the national hero who is a semi-outcast among his own people, but who saves them nonetheless. In the dying months of Nazi Germany, selbstopfereinsatz missions were flown by Luftwaffe pilots against Soviet bridgeheads on the Oder.[31] In 1950, Cecil B. DeMille used Jabotinsky's novel as the basis for his film Samson and Delilah. And a still more recent example is the film Armageddon, in which a group of socially marginalised Americans sacrifice their lives by detonating their spacecraft inside a comet that is on a collision course with Earth. In doing so they are defying tradition and even lawful orders, but they earn thereby the eternal gratitude of their people. As Robert Jewett and John Lawrence have shown, this image of the American hero as the ordinary man impatient of traditional authority who risks or destroys himself to save the world (John Brown, Charles Bronson, Sylvester Stallone, Captain America, Superman, Spiderman, and Captain Picard in the final episode of Star Trek), is the great monomyth of today's West.[32] In some Eastern parts, the popularity of magically vanishing Bin Laden figures, who emerge from undistinguished lives to break conventional laws in order to save the world, offers another suggestion of how deeply Westernised Arab culture has become.

Let no-one claim, then, that suicide bombing is alien to the West. It is a recurrent possibility of Europe's heritage. What needs emphasizing, against the snapshot thinking of the journalists, is the absence of a parallel strand in Islamic thinking. For Islam, suicide is always forbidden; some regard it as worse than murder.[33] Many Biblical stories are retold by Islam, but the idea of suicidal militancy is entirely absent from the scriptures. Saul's suicide is not present in the Koran, nor do we find it in Tabari's great *Annals* (which wish simply to record that he died in battle).[34] The Koranic Jonah does not ask to be pitched overboard, and Job does not pray for death. Similarly, the suicidal *istishhad* of Samson is absent from the Koran and Hadith, no doubt in line with their insistence on the absolute wickedness of suicide. The same Islamic idealism that cannot accept David's seduction of Bathsheba, or Lot's incest, has here airbrushed out Samson's killing of the innocent and his self-destruction.

Again, the point is clear: the scriptural and antique sensibilities which provided some cultural space for suicidal warfare in Western civilisation appear to have very thin foundations in Islam. Flying into a skyscraper to save the world is closer to the line which links Samson to Captain America, with a detour through the Book of Revelation, than to any Muslim conception of *futuwwa*.

Here are Buruma and Margalit, in their important study of Westernised anti-Westernism:

> Bin Laden's use of the word 'insane' is more akin to the Nazis' constant use of *fanatisch*. Human sacrifice is not an established Muslim tradition. Holy war always was justified in defence of the Islamic state, and believers who died in battle were promised heavenly delights, but glorification of death for its own sake was not part of this, especially in the Sunni tradition. [...] And the idea that freelance terrorists would enter paradise as martyrs by murdering unarmed civilians is a modern invention, one that would have horrified Muslims in the past. Islam is not a death cult.[35]

The irony of an Islamism with Western roots is one of the bitter
tragedies of our times, and many on both sides will deny it furi-
ously; yet the symptoms of this parasitic xenophobia are not far
to seek. One may readily be detected in a shared fondness for
conspiracy theories. The messianic importance of the hidden
deliverer is emphasised by the machinations of the forces of
darkness which are ranged against him. The mu'amara, or Plot,
is everywhere, as Robert Fisk, that dauntless lamentor of
Mid-East fantasies, regularly observes.[36] A sadly typical example
is given by Abdelwahab Meddeb:

> When I was at Abu Dhabi in May 2001, a number of my inter-
> locutors, of various Arab communities (Lebanese, Syrian,
> Sudanese, etc.), confirmed the warning, spread by the local
> newspapers, to the public of the countries of the Near East not
> to buy the very inexpensive belts with the label Made in Thailand.
> These belts, the people told me, were actually Israeli products in
> disguise and carried a kind of flea that propagated an incurable
> disease: one more Zionist trick to weaken Arab bodies, if not
> eliminate them. These interlocutors, otherwise reasonable and
> likable, gave credit to information as fantastic as that. Those are
> the fantasies in which the symptoms of the sickness of Islam
> can be seen, the receptive compost in which the crime of
> September 11 could be welcomed joyfully.[37]

Again, this is a historical aberration for Muslims. Healthy
communities far from Western influence find it incredible. The
current prevalence of a kind of Islamic McCarthyism, often
hysterical in its attempts to reduce a complex and enraging
modernity to a monomaniac opposition, is simply another
indication of how far the Islamists have travelled from the
tradition. Religion makes us more attentive to reality, while
secularity, bereft of real disciplines of self-knowledge and
self-disdain, permits a dream-self. 'They think that every shout

is against themselves,' says the Koran of the hypocrites (63:4), while praising the believers for their clearsighted faith that only God is powerful, and it is only He that should be feared. The correct mindset is specified in scripture:

> Those to whom the people said: 'The people have gathered against you, therefore fear them!' But it increased them in faith, and they said: 'Allah is enough for us, an excellent Guardian is he!'
> So they returned with grace and favour from Allah, and no harm touched them. They followed the good-pleasure of Allah, and Allah is of great bounty.
> It is only the devil who would make [men] fear his allies. Fear them not; fear Me, if you are believers. (3:173–5)

The context is the aftermath of Uhud, when waverers warned of the strength of the combined enemies around Medina. Paranoia thus becomes the marker of imperfect faith and undue respect for the *asbab*. But despair is *kufr*: Islam's Samson could never say:

> Hopeless are all my evils, all remediless;
> This one prayer yet remains, might I be heard,
> No long petition, speedy death,
> The close of all my miseries, and the balm.[38]

Further, it requires an apparently unbearable humility for the Islamist conspiracy theorist to recognise that until very recently Muslims have seldom been perceived by the United States as a noteworthy enemy. For most of its history, America has opposed and feared and stereotyped Englishmen, Rebels, Red Indians, Spaniards, Huns, Reds or Gooks. The current preoccupation with Muslims is shallow in the US memory, if we discount the brief and long-forgotten enthusiasms of the Decatur episode.

Again, as with the conspiracy theories which urgently needed to see 9/11 as the work of Mossad, and the utilitarian justification of the vanguard's suspension of the ethical, the radical Islamists are an expression of the very Westernising alienation they profess to defy. In a sense, the West hates them because they are more modern than itself, and thus remind it of the unbearable risks it has taken by following the road of Enlightenment. As Meddeb reminds us: 'Who are those who died while spreading death in New York, Washington and Pennsylvania? [...] They are the sons of our times, the pure products of the Americanisation of the world.'[39]

Self-immolation in Gaza to bring down the unbelieving temple. This is tragedy in Wagnerian mode. It is suicide, *selbstmord*, not really prefatory to redemption, but to publicity and therapy. It was Nietzsche, not any Islamic sage, who wrote: 'The thought of suicide is a great source of comfort: with it a calm passage is to be made across many a bad night.'[40] After being 'eyeless in Gaza, at the mill with slaves,' Samson experiences 'calm of mind, all passion spent'[41] – the English idiom begins with Milton's ending, linking, as do some readings of the Samson legend, *eros* and *thanatos*, desire and death.

But it is Nietzsche who introduces the modern superhero. If 'the splendrous blond beast, avidly rampant for plunder and victory' cannot take the revenge which heals his heart, he will end his unworthy existence in a magnificent, Hitlerian funeral pyre. Samson thus becomes not a throwback, but an *anticipation* of modernity.

Religion, if it has the right to exist at all, must consider this a spurious healing. Neither vainglory nor despair can have a place in the metabolism of a religion based on the idea of God's unique mastery of history, the polar opposite of dualistic paganism, or of the romantic Enlightenment dream which found its tragic moods congenial. The scriptures denounce *hamiyya*, the feverish identity-politics of the pagan Arabs; the post-orthodox Islamist admits it to his heart. 'Roots of Muslim Rage' is the title of Bernard Lewis' most notorious piece on Islamism.[42] His pathology of the roots is far astray; but the rage is undeniable. How are we to understand such rage in the heart of a religion built on submission to the Divine will, *hulwihi wa-murrihi*, the bitter and the sweet of it? Which insisted that 'it is not the wrestler who is strong; it is the man who masters himself when angry'?[43] Why did the Blessed Prophet pray for 'a certainty by which You render slight in our eyes the calamities of this world'?[44]

The roots are, as it turns out, instrumental reason, natural causality, and the enthroning of Aristotle over Plato, or Newton over St Denys. Without the certainty of an omnipotent God (and is not Islam here better at restraining passion than all other faiths?) the experience of adversity leaves us prey to wild emotion. It was this same *jahili* craving for revenge that led Churchill astray, as one historian suggests: 'In this superheated and bloody time emotion may have masqueraded as political thinking in a rationalizing Prime Minister's mind.'[45]

Religion is never more tested than when our emotions are ablaze. At such a time, the timeless grandeur of the Law and its ethics stand at our mercy. 'Let the qadi not judge when he is angry,' as it is said. But here is the reality of Gaza:

> 'Hamas operations are not directed and have never been directed against children,' says Hamas political leader Ismail Abu Shanaab. 'It is directed at military targets.' When pushed, however, he goes further. 'To be frank with you, there are a lot of the moralities which got broken in this war,' he says. 'They are letting the Israelis kill Palestinians and they want the Palestinians to be moderate, to be moral. We cannot control the game because it has no rules, it has no limits.'[46]

Revenge, rage, the teleological suspension of the ethical. It is Churchillian, but also aromatic with a not-yet-dispersed

Marxism. Here, for instance, is Mawdudi, a tributary of the
Hamas vision:

> 'Muslim' is the name of the international revolutionary party
> which Islam organizes to implement its revolutionary program
> and Jihad is that revolutionary struggle which the Islamic party
> carries out to achieve its objectives.[47]

As Abdullah Schleifer goes on to remark:

> Mawdoodi took as his enduring model a progression of
> dynamic relationships – the movement, the party, revolutionary
> struggle, the revolution – defined by one of the major desacral-
> izing forces in contemporary times, in pursuit of a concept of
> state that draws its substance from non-Islamic sources, and all
> with that same innocence of the modern Muslim importing his
> 'value-free' technology.[48]

The antinomian quality of this furious insurrectionist method
confirms Gray's suggestion that Islamism is simply another
modern weapon against religion. For theists, the ethical can
never be suspended; on the contrary, it is needed most when
most under strain. Yet the militant transgressions of radicals form
only part of a much wider picture of covert but deep surrender to
Enlightenment thought.

Islamism, that *soi-disant* hammer of the Franks, is ironically
modern in very many ways. It is modern in its eagerness for
science and its hatred of 'superstition.' It is modern in its
rejection of all higher spirituality (Qutb recommends, instead,
'*al-fana' fi'l-'aqida*').[49] It is modern in its rejection of the principle
of tradition, and, despite itself, cannot but impose the
insecurities of Western-trained minds (and are they not all
engineers and doctors?) on scripture. Intertextuality and the
community of sages are barred. The theopolitics of classical

Islam, where both scholarship and the state are invigorated by mutual tension (the Men of the Pen and the Men of the Sword), is replaced by the finally Western model of the ideological totalitarian state, with a self-appointed clerisy (albeit composed of technocrats) requiring absolute control over policy and the Shari'a. The modular diversities of pre-modern Muslim societies, where villages, tribes, and millat minorities regulated themselves, give way to the Islamist appropriation of the machinery of centralised post-colonial étatism. Social subsets which flourished for centuries under, say, Ottomanism, already eroded by centralising colonial regimes, are finally liquidated by a vision that is purely Western, albeit camouflaged by loud religious language. As Maryam Jameelah puts it, in a courageous article in which she publicly announces her disillusionment with the Islamist model:

> The tragic paradox of the life and thought of Maulana Sayyid Abul Ala Mawdoodi was his subconscious acceptance of the very same Western ideas he dedicated his entire life to struggling against.[50]

In such a system, those who should be serving God end up obeying the men of the state who are His all too fallible interpreters. They worship in fear of the police, not in fear of God. Dissidence becomes a simultaneous treason and blasphemy. The failure of this totalitarian-model of the 'Islamic State', this 'carceral Islamism' which makes a Muslim land a prison rather than a landscape of options and regional variety, is today everywhere apparent, and is a sign, perhaps, that God will not allow victory to such a perversion. For the Muslims will not long be allowed to bow before any other than God.

V

DIES IRAE

IS THIS ATTACK on tradition a modernity with a future? Zealotry itself is not normally refuted, it has to subside. Economic failure provoked a crisis of Soviet faith. Military disaster at the hands of *üntermenschen* pulled the rug from beneath the feet of Nazism. And where material failure does not produce a subsidence, it is enabled by schism: Cromwell could not be replicated because of the powerfully fissiparous quality of Dissent. Calvin's Geneva hardly outlived him. Hutterites, Levellers, Anabaptists, and the other fragments of the Protestant detonation could perpetuate themselves, but their energy source seemed to have a half-life. Islamic extremism, what has historically been called *ghuluww*, excess, and has occasionally, though not often, troubled the religion's equilibrium, usually knows a similar deflation through internal factionalism and the disappointment which seeps into all annunciatory movements when the world does not either improve or come to an end. In the case of Muslim puritanism, we see, currently, infighting, as in Algeria, and on the streets of Riyadh. Apathy may not be long postponed.

This seems likely, to the extent that Islamism is the product of indigenous decay, a second Reformation. But will its porosity to Enlightenment thought prolong or accelerate this decay? (How ironic that Islam's Reformation should come *after* its Enlightenment!) Here predictions about Islamism may not be so

37

different from predictions about a certain kind of exhibitionist postmodernism. Take Foucault, for instance. On his death, he had been praised by *Le Monde* as 'the most important event of thought in our century.' He was an iconic Western iconoclast, but more honest about the consequences of modernity than most liberal seekers after virtue. He had been strongly pro-Khomeini, and had also praised the Baader-Meinhof terrorists. Like many Islamists, he was a lapsed Marxist, concerned with making a statement, with angering the middle-class West, with disruption. A second Bakunin, he was concerned not with advancing a detailed and realistic agenda, but with a passionate desire to shock. And like his hero Nietzsche, he died of a venereal disease, his immensely careless sexual habits indicating the powerful allure of suicide for the sake of making a statement. We need to ask: is this too close for comfort to radical Islamism, with its penchant for *épater les blancs* by whatever means? For how long can the West portray the Islamists as its own polar opposite? Will it be harder to forget the zealots than to forget Foucault?

This is less hopeful: Foucault has not been forgotten. The ambient vacuum which permitted a philosophy of the absurd in France and in the Middle East shows no signs of abatement. Capitalist shortsightedness wedded to postmodern philosophy may offer the only real life-support system that the Muslim reformation can hope for. Thus the defeat of the Muslim aberration may depend on nothing less than the defeat of the current global system, and its replacement with an order grounded in the ethical brilliance of the monotheisms. This diagnosis places us far beyond both Qutb's chauvinism and the narcissism of the neocons. The same classical Islamic strength through cosmopolitanism that helped our ancient order to endure as a non-totalitarian expression of certainty must be remobilised to affirm the Other's heart, in order to reconnect the global system with religious reality. That is, a successful 'war on terror' cannot be detached from a humanly consensual war on environmental loss, on unfair trade, on identity feminism, and on genetic manipulation. If it is so detached, it will be lost.

Blake portrays the spirit of the industrial age as Urizen, blind ignorance, fettered in laws of causality unveiled by Newton, and sunk in feral emotionalism. Religion is indispensable to the nurturing of a true humanism because it fights this, and insists that humanity has a *telos*, and that the soul is therefore sacrosanct.

To succeed, then we must be able to realise that self-judgement, that greatest and most irreplaceable gift of the Abrahamic religions, is more than an evolutionary confidence trick. Consider Jürgen Habermas' latest book, which reflects on human nature as challenged by genetic science.[1] Postmodernism seems to problematise self-judgement; and its associated ethical practice seems to reduce Aristotle's greatness of soul, which he, against later monotheist reaction, considered a virtue, to *superbia*, greatest of the seven deadly sins. But Habermas reminds us that confronted by genetic science, we are required, after a long hiatus, to judge ourselves. For science seeks our permission to rebuild our bodies to reduce the suffering of future generations; yet in the process it must ask us to define what we presently are. Liberal ethics, which resist both such definitions, and any exercise in using human beings for our own purposes, however idealistic, are thereby interrogated. Habermas is quite clear that the West's conception of virtue is a Christian ghost, rooted in a Kantianism that has been the basis of liberal notions of individual autonomy. Yet he seems convinced that this ghost still lives, and can be maintained perpetually, and may even serve as the stable basis of ever more ambitious projects for universal codes of human rights, in the arena of bioethics, as elsewhere. This will include, presumably, the war on Carrelian Islamism.

John Gray, iconoclastically again, is unsure that this is as coherent as it is helpful. Gray, whose understanding of Al-Qaida as an Enlightenment project we noted earlier, would rather we revisited Schopenhauer's deconstruction of Kant. Frightened ethicists have deceived themselves that there is no Christianity in this Christian ghost. Yet true Kantianism would reject the categoric imperative as a false projection upon the Noumenon. Our desperate desire to find a new moral anchorage after the sinking of Christian scholasticism blinds us to what is for Gray the unanswerable insight that without God, we are beyond good and evil. Schopenhauer saw, as Gray put it, 'that the enlightenment was only a secular version of Christianity's central mistake.'[2] There is no soul, only the individual will, and we have no reason to suppose that we are any more free in our decision-making than the animals from which religion taught us that we were so categorically distinct. Our consciousness is just one more part of the world. Heidegger turns out to be worse: he insists that he excludes Christian paradigms, but internalises them implicitly in his consideration of the human plight, suffering, guilt, and the paradox of being. And while Schopenhauer maintained a pure and private pessimism, Heidegger sought to intuit Being in his tribe. 'The Führer himself and alone,' he exclaimed, 'is the present and future German reality and its law.' Hitler's xenophobia allowed the philosopher to repair his wounds, and reconnect with Being. Qutbian fundamentalism is not far away.

It is impossible to exaggerate the debt Giddens' 'runaway world' owes to Christianity, for showing so much vitality even after Nietzsche proclaimed the death of its God. But for the Gospels, the Western empire would not have benefited from Kant's conjuring trick, or Rawls' benign adversion to 'good people'. Yet the fact of its precariousness remains; and the risk of a tribal resolution is enormous.[3] Science harnessed to *Geist* dragged up Hitler; and something similar has beset Islam. Solidarity, mythologically voiced, technologically imposed, is to be the cure for our desperate alienation. Remember the words of the Furies in Aeschylus:

For many ills one attitude is the cure
When it agrees on what to hate.[4]

The danger, then, is that liberalism will prove too weak to prevent one form of Enlightenment chauvinism – carceral Islamism – from triggering a sudden revival of another such form – Hitlerian essentialism. The prosperity of the far-right across the liberal West shows how far this march has already come. Postmodernity is methodologically incapable of resisting this; and monotheism must step into the breach. A monotheism, however, which bears all the arms it has acquired and sharpened during its travels: its intellectual appropriation of Athens, its hospitality to the autochthonously non-Semitic, its insistence on diversity, all enabled and preserved by the centrality of spiritual purgation. The civil war within Enlightenment modernity that Gray identifies as the essence of the 'war on terror' is suicidal. Only a *ressourcement* in the anchored past can deliver us.

NOTES

I. AMNESIA

1. Cited in John Gray, *Straw Dogs: thoughts on humans and other animals* (London, 2002), 75.
2. Daniel Dennett, *Consciousness Explained* (London, 1992); Daniel Wegner, *The Illusion of Conscious Will* (Bradford, 2002).
3. *The Lark Ascending*.
4. For the neocons see Stefan Halper and Jonathan Clarke, *America Alone: The Neo-Conservatives and the Global Order* (Cambridge, 2004).
5. Cited in Robert Jewett and John Shelton Lawrence, *Captain America and the Crusade against Evil: The Dilemma of Zealous Nationalism* (Grand Rapids and Cambridge, 2003), 131.

II. SUNNA CONTRA GENTILES

1. Daniel Jonah Goldhagen, *A Moral Reckoning: The Role of the Catholic Church in the Holocaust and its Unfulfilled Duty of Repair* (London: 2002), 369–70; e.g. 'The Catholic Church and other Christian churches [...] could include in every Christian Bible a detailed, corrective account alongside the text about its many antisemitic passages, and a clear disclaimer explaining that even though these passages were once presented as fact, they are actually false or dubious and have been the source of much unjust injury. They could include essays on the various failings of the Christian Bible,

and a detailed running commentary on each page that would correct the texts' erroneous and libellous assertions.'

2. Cf. Julia Lipton, 'Othello Circumcised: Shakespeare and the Pauline Discourse of Nations', *Representations* 57 (1997), 78: 'Christian typologists also used Esau, Pharoah and Herod to couple the Jew and the Muslim as carnal children of Abraham facing each other across the world-historical break effected by the Incarnation.'

3. See Fukuyama: 'A country that makes human rights a significant element of its foreign policy tends toward ineffectual moralizing at best, and unconstrained violence in pursuit of moral aims at worst.' *Harper's Magazine*, August 2001, p. 36.

4. Salah Abd al-Fattah al-Khalidi, *Amrika min al-dakhil bi-minzar Sayyid Qutb* (Beirut, 2002).

5. Roxanne L. Euben, *Enemy in the Mirror: Islamic Fundamentalism and the Limits of Modern Rationalism* (Princeton, 1999), 52; citing Qutb's *Khasa'is al-Tasawwur al-Islami*; Youssef Choueiri, *Islamic Fundamentalism* (London 1990), 142–9. As Choueiri concludes: 'What Qutb fails to inform his vanguard, however, is that the code of conduct he subsequently elaborated in his 'commentary' on the Koran matches that of Carrel much more than Muhammad's own Traditions.' The result is not an indigenous form of governance, but 'a Third World version of Fascism.'

6. Samuel Goitein, *Jews and Arabs* (New York, 1955), 130: 'Never has Judaism encountered such a close and fructuous symbiosis as that with the medieval civilization of Arab Islam.'

7. Many Muslims who have rejected the new radicalism in favour of authenticity will sympathise with the experience of Franky Schaeffer, who in the 1970s was an extreme Calvinist advocate of totalitarian government. In the 1980s, shocked by the reality of fundamentalist leaders, he joined the Greek Orthodox Church, denouncing the Protestant radicals as 'a hybrid composed of fragments of ancient Christian faith and thoroughly modern, anti-traditional, materialist and often utopian ideas.' Cited in Steve Bruce, *Fundamentalism* (Cambridge, 2000), 122.

8. John Gray, *Al-Qaeda and What it Means to be Modern* (London, 2003), 1–2.

9. Slavoj Zizek, *Welcome to the Desert of the Real* (London and New York: Verso, 2002), 146.

10. See for instance Richard Martin, 'The Religious Foundations of War, Peace and Statecraft in Islam', in John Kelsay and James Turner Johnson (eds), *Just War and Jihad: Historical and Theoretical Perspectives on War and Peace in Western and Islamic Traditions.* (New York, Westport and London, 1991.)

11. *Naqd Kalam al-Shaykh al-Albani fi Sharitihi Min Manhaj al-Khawarij.* N.d., n.p.

12. L. Carl Brown, *Religion and State: the Muslim approach to politics* (New York, 2000), 156–7. It needs to be added that Qutb's aberration is typical of those who carry out radical ijtihad without the needful qualifications in shari'a sciences. For instance, he develops his absolutist rejection of any conversation with the West in his *Ma'alim fi'l-tariq* (Cairo, 1980), 145, on the basis of out-of-context Koranic verses (2:109, 2:120, and 3:100), which warn only of the dangers of cooperating with *some* of the *ahl al-kitab*. To try and force the issue, he then produces a hadith from Abu Ya'la, 'Do not ask the People of the Book about anything ...' (Abu Ya'la, *Musnad* [Damascus and Beirut, 1985/1405], IV, 102), apparently unaware that this hadith is weak; see 'Abduh 'Ali Kushak, *al-Maqsad al-A'la fi taqrib ahadith al-Hafiz Abi Ya'la* (Beirut, 1422/2001), I, 83. In any case, who is more absurd than the radical who rejects all Western influence, and then writes books with titles like *Khasa'is al-Tasawwur al-Islami* ('Special Qualities of the Islamic Conception')? Qutb's whole manner of expression would be unimaginable without modernity.

13. Abdelwahab Meddeb, *Islam and its discontents* (London, 2003), 48–52. Qutb's waning interest in literature is one symptom of this.

14. Abu Hamid al-Ghazali, *Disciplining the Soul*, tr. T. Winter (Cambridge, 1995), 86.

15. 'Asian Muslims in particular have come to reify the shari'a as much as any Orientalist, converting the law into a symbol of ethnic

identification.' Lawrence Rosen, *The Justice of Islam: Comparative perspectives on Islamic law and society* (Oxford, 2000), 186.

16. www.dfw.com/mld/bayarea/news/6281132.htm?1c

III. JUS IN BELLO

1. W. G. Sebald, *On the Natural History of Destruction* (London, 2004), 17.
2. Stephen A. Garrett, *Ethics and airpower in World War II: the British bombing of German cities* (New York and Basingstoke, 1993), 28.
3. Garrett, 90; Harvey Tress, *British strategic bombing through 1940: politics, attitudes, and the formation of a lasting pattern* (Lewiston, 1988), 304.
4. Garrett, 90.
5. Garrett, 103.
6. Tress, 335.
7. Cited in Garrett, 20.
8. Cited in Garrett, 132.
9. Garrett, 96.
10. General Curtis LeMay, who planned the Tokyo attacks which killed perhaps a hundred thousand civilians, remarked that they were 'scorched and boiled and baked to death.' (John W. Dower, *War Without Mercy: Race and Power in the Pacific War* [New York, 1986], 50.)
11. Menahem Begin, *The Revolt* (revised edition, London 1979), 59–60.

IV. SAMSON TERRORISTES

1. A substantial literature now exists seeking to identify suicide bombing as a paradigmatically Muslim act. See, for instance, Shaul Shay, *The Shahids: Islam and Suicide Attacks* (Transaction, 2003); also Christoph Reuter, *My Life is a Weapon: A Modern History of Suicide Bombing* (Princeton, 2004). This forms part of a larger determination to show the radicals as authentic expressions of Islamic tradition (see, for instance, the works of Emmanuel Sivan). The level of Islamic knowledge present in this literature is

usually poor; see for instance Reuter's belief (p. 22) that the Mu'tazilites were founded by Ibn Sina and Ibn Rushd! Reuter is a *Stern* journalist, whose patronage by Princeton University Press shows the fragility of the standards of American academic institutions in times of international crisis.

2. Sir James Frazier, *The Golden Bough. Part III: The Dying God* (London, 1913), 42. For a more recent study see Jacques Gernet, 'Les suicides par le feu chez les bouddhiques chinoises de Ve au Xe siecle', *Mélanges publiés par l'Institut des Hautes Études Chinoises* I (1960), 527–558. For Buddhist suicide in India see W. Rahula, 'Self-Cremation in Mahayana Buddhism' in his *Zen and the Taming of the Bull* (London, 1978), 111–6. Rahula amplifies (p. 113): 'Usually a self-cremation was done in public, but there were some monks who burnt themselves secretly. One monk burnt himself in a cauldron of oil. Some made a modest offering to a *stupa* by cutting off a finger or a hand, wrapping it with cloth drenched in oil, and setting fire to it.' The practice is traced back to the time of the Buddha himself; as F. Woodward records: 'The Buddha approved of the suicide of bhikkus; but in these cases they were Arahants, and we are to suppose that such beings who have mastered self, can do what they please as regards the life and death of their carcases' ('The Ethics of Suicide in Greek, Latin and Buddhist Literature', *Buddhist Annual of Ceylon* [1922], p. 8).

3. Ibid, 54. See also the ritual described on page 47, in which the king of Calicut 'had to cut his throat in public at the end of a twelve years' reign.'

4. Upendra Thakur, *The History of Suicide in India: An Introduction* (Delhi, 1963), xv–xvi.

5. Ibid., 9. See also the section on 'Religious Suicide', on pp. 77–111.

6. *Rihlat Ibn Battuta* (Beirut, 1379/1960), 411–3, focussing on the practice of bride-burning, but referring also to Hindu self-drowning rituals. See also Muhammad ibn Ahmad al-Biruni, *Tahqiq ma li'l-Hind* (Hyderabad, 1377/1958), p. 480: 'Those among them who kill themselves do so during eclipses; or they may hire a man to drown

them in the Ganges. Such people hold them underwater until they die.' For more on this practice see Thakur, 112.

7. Edgar O'Ballance, *The Cyanide War: Tamil Insurrection in Sri Lanka 1973–88* (London, 1989), p. 13, for the first Tamil suicide martyrs in the 1970s. Other Tamil Tiger terrorist habits include beheading (p. 10), taking Western hostages (p. 40), and drug-dealing to fund operations (p. 120).

8. For the religious puritanism of the Tamil Tigers (no extramarital relations, no alcohol, etc.), see Dagmar Hellmann-Rajayanagar, *The Tamil Tigers: armed struggle for identity* (Stuttgart, 1994), 37. Sometimes considered to be Marxist, the Tamil Tigers are primarily inspired by national and religious tradition (ibid., p. 56).

9. Amantha Perera, 'Suicide bombers feared and revered,' *Asia Times*, July 17, 2003. For more on Islamist borrowings from Tamil suicide warfare see Amy Waldman, 'Masters of Suicide Bombing: Tamil Guerillas of Sri Lanka' (*New York Times*, 14 January 2003).

10. Cf. Plotinus, against the Stoics: 'if each man's rank in the other world depends on his state when he goes out, one must not take out the soul as long as there is any possibility of progress' (Ennead I.9; cf. also the Elias fragment of Plotinus found after this section in Armstrong's Loeb translation). This is similar to the Islamic virtue of praying for a long life in the service of God. (Ibn Hanbal, *Musnad*, VI, 23.)

11. 'Within Israelite society, as early as the period of the united monarchy, voluntary death, given the proper circumstances, was understood as honorable and even routine.' (Arthur J. Droge and James D. Tabor, *Noble Death: Suicide and Martyrdom among Christians and Jews in antiquity* [San Francisco, 1992], 56.)

12. See J. W. van Henten, *The Maccabean martyrs as saviours of the Jewish people: a study of 2 and 4 Maccabees* (Leiden and New York, 1997).

13. Droge and Tabor, 87, 100. See also Sidney Hoenig, 'The Sicarii in Masada – Glory or Infamy?' *Tradition* 11 (1970), 5–30; Sidney Goldstein, *Suicide in Rabbinic Literature* (Hoboken, 1989), 41–2.

14. Daniel Boyarin, *Dying for God: Martyrdom and the Making of Christianity and Judaism* (Stanford, 1999), 171. It is not insignificant that 'during the Moslem period, mass suicides among Jews do not seem to have occurred' (Goldstein, 49).

15. The former Ashkenazy Chief Rabbi of Israel, Shlomo Goren, allowed suicide as an alternative to prisoner-of-war status, following the examples of Saul and Masada (Goldstein, 49).

16. Walter S. Wurzburger, *Ethics of Responsibility: Pluralistic Approaches to Covenantal Ethics* (Philadelphia, 1994), 92. For more, see Goldstein's chapter entitled 'Suicide as an Act of Martyrdom', pp. 41–50.

17. 'In strictly historical terms it is unlikely that Jesus of Nazareth ever expected to give his life as "a ransom for many" (Mark 10:45). Rather, his intention was to bring about the restoration of Israel and to usher in the kingdom of God.' (Droge and Tabor, 115.) Islam would probably be more impressed by the Lucan Jesus, who apparently never intended to die.

18. Droge and Tabor, 136.

19. Droge and Tabor, 134–9, 152–5; 167–83. Voluntary martyrdom continued in some places, such as early Muslim Cordova, where 48 Christians were beheaded between 850 and 859: 'the majority of the victims deliberately invoked capital punishment by publicly blaspheming Muhammad and disparaging Islam.' They were eulogised by the Church. (K. B. Wolf, *Christian Martyrs in Muslim Spain* [Cambridge, 1988], 1.)

20. Frazier, 45.

21. Glen Bowersock, *Martyrdom and Rome* (Cambridge, 1995), 66–7.

22. Brian Wicker, 'Samson Terroristes: A Theological Reflection on Suicidal Terrorism', *New Blackfriars*, vol. 84 no. 983 (January 2003), 45. I am indebted to Wicker for much of the information in the next two paragraphs.

23. Bernhard Anderson, *The Living World of the Old Testament* (London, 1958), 111.

24. Droge and Tabor, 186.

25. John Milton, *Poetical Works* (Edinburgh, 1853), II, 76.
26. Milton, 125.
27. Vladimir Jabotinsky, *Prelude to Delilah* (New York, 1945), 131. This is a translation of the original, published as *Samson* in 1926.
28. Jabotinsky, 330.
29. Jabotinsky, 200.
30. Stephen Rosenfeld, 'Straight to the Heart of Menachem Begin', *Present Tense* (Summer 1980), 7.
31. Antony Beevor, *Berlin 1945, the downfall.* (London, 2002), 238. Focke-Wulf fighter-bombers packed with explosives would deliberately ram Soviet bridges and command centres.
32. Jewett and Lawrence, 35–9.
33. 'Abdallah ibn Qutayba, *'Uyun al-akhbar* (Cairo, 1348/1930), iii, 217.
34. Tabari, *History, Volume III: The Children of Israel*, translated by William M. Brinner (Albany, 1991), 139.
35. I. Buruma and A. Margalit, *Occidentalism: A Short History of Anti-Westernism* (London, 2004), 68–9.
36. Robert Fisk, *Pity the Nation: Lebanon at War* (London, 1990), 78, 79, 85, 139, 166, 175, 178, 302, 320, 374, 408, 523, 530, 567, 603.
37. Meddeb, 115.
38. Milton, 93.
39. Meddeb, 9.
40. Friedrich Nietzsche, *Beyond Good and Evil*, tr. Helen Zimmern (London, 1907, repr.1967), 98.
41. Milton, 126.
42. Bernard Lewis, 'Roots of Muslim Rage,' *The Atlantic Monthly*, September 1990.
43. Bukhari and Muslim from Abu Hurayra.
44. Tirmidhi and al-Hakim (1, 528), from Ibn 'Umar.
45. Tress, 289.
46. http://news.bbc.co.uk/1/hi/world/middle_east/2179606.stm
47. Cited by S. Abdullah Schleifer, 'Jihad: Sacred Struggle in Islam IV,' *The Islamic Quarterly* 28/ii (1984), 98.
48. Schleifer, 100.

49. William E. Shepard, *Sayyid Qutb and Islamic Activism: A Translation and Critical Annotation of Social Justice in Islam* (Leiden, 1996), p. xxxiii. Here we have, again, the phenomenon of 'loving the Torah more than God'.
50. Maryam Jameelah, 'An Appraisal of Some Aspects of the Life and Thought of Maulana Sayyid Abul Ala Maududi', *Islamic Quarterly* xxxi (1407–1987), 116–130, p. 130.

V. DIES IRAE

1. Jürgen Habermas, *The Future of Human Nature* (London: 2003).
2. Gray, *Straw Dogs*, 41.
3. See Gray, *Straw Dogs*, 102–3: 'The egalitarian beliefs on which Rawls's theory is founded are like the sexual mores that were once believed to be the core of morality. The most local and changeable of things, they are revered as the very essence of morality. As conventional opinion moves on, the current egalitarian consensus will be followed by a new orthodoxy, equally certain that it embodies unchanging moral truth.'
4. *The Eumenides*, 996–7.

BIBLIOGRAPHY

'Abduh 'Ali Kushak. *al-Maqsad al-a'la fi taqrib ahadith al-hafiz Abi Ya'la*. vol. 1. Beirut, 1422/2001.

Abu Ya'la. *Musnad*. Damascus and Beirut, 1985/1405. 4:102.

al-Biruni, Muhammad ibn Ahmad. *Tahqiq ma li'l-Hind*. Hyderabad, 1377/1958.

al-Ghazali, Abu Hamid. *Disciplining the Soul*. Translated by T. J. Winter. Cambridge, 1995.

al-Khalidi, Salah Abd al-Fattah. *Amrika min al-dakhil bi-minzar Sayyid Qutb*. Beirut, 2002.

Anderson, Bernhard. *The Living World of the Old Testament*. London, 1958.

Beevor, Antony. *Berlin 1945, the Downfall*. London, 2002.

Begin, Menahem. *The Revolt*. Revised edition. London, 1979.

Bowersock, Glen. *Martyrdom and Rome*. Cambridge, 1995.

Boyarin, Daniel. *Dying for God: Martyrdom and the Making of Christianity and Judaism*. Stanford, 1999.

Brown, L. Carl. *Religion and State: The Muslim Approach to Politics*. New York, 2000.

Bruce, Steve. *Fundamentalism*. Cambridge, 2000.

Buruma, I. and A. Margalit. *Occidentalism: A Short History of Anti-Westernism*. London, 2004.

Choueiri, Youssef. *Islamic Fundamentalism*. London, 1990.

Dennett, Daniel. *Consciousness Explained*. London, 1992.

Dower, John W. *War without Mercy: Race and Power in the Pacific War.* New York, 1986.

Droge, Arthur J. and James D. Tabor, *Noble Death: Suicide and Martyrdom among Christians and Jews in Antiquity.* San Francisco, 1992.

Euben, Roxanne L. *Enemy in the Mirror: Islamic Fundamentalism and the Limits of Modern Rationalism.* Princeton, 1999.

Fisk, Robert. *Pity the Nation: Lebanon at War.* London, 1990.

Frazier, Sir James. *The Golden Bough.* "Part 3: The Dying God." London, 1913.

Garrett, Stephen A. *Ethics and Airpower in World War II: The British Bombing of German Cities.* New York and Basingstoke, 1993.

Gernet, Jacques. "Les suicides par le feu chez les bouddhiques chinoises de Ve au Xe siecle." *Mélanges publiés par l'Institut des Hautes Études Chinoises* I (1960).

Goitein, Samuel. *Jews and Arabs.* New York, 1955.

Goldhagen, Daniel Jonah. *A Moral Reckoning: The Role of the Catholic Church in the Holocaust and its Unfulfilled Duty of Repair.* London, 2002.

Goldstein, Sidney. *Suicide in Rabbinic Literature.* Hoboken, 1989.

Gray, John. *Straw Dogs: Thoughts on Humans and Other Animals.* London, 2002.

Habermas, Jürgen. *The Future of Human Nature.* London, 2003.

Halper, Stefan and Jonathan Clarke. *America Alone: The Neo-Conservatives and the Global Order.* Cambridge, 2004.

Hellmann-Rajayanagar, Dagmar. *The Tamil Tigers: Armed Struggle for Identity.* Stuttgart, 1994.

Hoenig, Sidney. "The Sicarii in Masada—Glory or Infamy?" *Tradition* 11 (1970).

Ibn Hanbal. *Musnad.* N.p. VI, 23

Ibn Qutayba, 'Abdallah. '*Uyun al-akhbar.* Cairo, 1348/1930.

Jabotinsky, Vladimir. *Prelude to Delilah.* New York, 1945.

Jameelah, Maryam. "An Appraisal of Some Aspects of the Life and Thought of Maulana Sayyid Abul Ala Maududi." *Islamic Quarterly* 31 (1407/1987).

Jewett, Robert and John Shelton Lawrence. *Captain America and the Crusade against Evil: The Dilemma of Zealous Nationalism*. Grand Rapids and Cambridge, 2003.

Lewis, Bernard. "Roots of Muslim Rage." *Atlantic Monthly* (September 1990).

Lipton, Julia. "Othello Circumcised: Shakespeare and the Pauline Discourse of Nations," *Representations* 57 (1997).

Martin, Richard. "The Religious Foundations of War, Peace and Statecraft in Islam." In *Just War and Jihad: Historical and Theoretical Perspectives on War and Peace in Western and Islamic Traditions*, edited by John Kelsay and James Turner Johnson. New York, Westport, and London, 1991.

Meddeb, Abdelwahab. *Islam and its Discontents*. London, 2003.

Milton, John. *Poetical Works*. Edinburgh, 1853. II.

Naqd kalam al-Shaykh al-Albani fi sharitihi min manhaj al-khawarij. N.d., n.p.

Nietzsche, Friedrich. *Beyond Good and Evil*. Translated by Helen Zimmern. London, 1907. Reprint 1967.

O'Ballance, Edgar. *The Cyanide War: Tamil Insurrection in Sri Lanka 1973–88*. London, 1989.

Perera, Amantha. "Suicide bombers feared and revered." *Asia Times*, 17 July 2003.

Rahula, W. "Self-Cremation in Mahayana Buddhism" in *Zen and the Taming of the Bull*. London, 1978.

Reuter, Christoph. *My Life is a Weapon: A Modern History of Suicide Bombing*. Princeton, 2004.

Rihlat Ibn Battuta. Beirut, 1379/1960.

Rosen, Lawrence. *The Justice of Islam: Comparative Perspectives on Islamic Law and Society*. Oxford, 2000.

Rosenfeld, Stephen. "Straight to the Heart of Menachem Begin." *Present Tense* (Summer 1980).

Schleifer, S. Abdullah. "Jihad: Sacred Struggle in Islam 4." *Islamic Quarterly* 28 (1984).

Sebald, W. G. *On the Natural History of Destruction*. London, 2004.

Shay, Shaul. *The Shahids: Islam and Suicide Attacks*. Np., Transaction, 2003.

Shepard, William E. *Sayyid Qutb and Islamic Activism: A Translation and Critical Annotation of Social Justice in Islam*. Leiden, 1996.

Tabari, *History*. Vol. 3 *The Children of Israel*. Translated by William M. Brinner. Albany, 1991.

Thakur, Upendra. *The History of Suicide in India: An Introduction*. Delhi, 1963.

Tress, Harvey. *British Strategic Bombing through 1940: Politics, Attitudes, and the Formation of a Lasting Pattern*. Lewiston, 1988.

van Henten, J. W. *The Maccabean Martyrs as Saviours of the Jewish People: A study of 2 and 4 Maccabees*. Leiden and New York, 1997.

Waldman, Amy. "Masters of Suicide Bombing: Tamil Guerillas of Sri Lanka" *New York Times*, 14 January 2003.

Wegner, Daniel. *The Illusion of Conscious Will*. Bradford, 2002.

Wicker, Brian. "Samson Terroristes: A Theological Reflection on Suicidal Terrorism." *New Blackfriars*. Vol. 84, no. 983 (January 2003).

Wolf, K. B. *Christian Martyrs in Muslim Spain*. Cambridge, 1988.

Woodward, F. "The Ethics of Suicide in Greek, Latin and Buddhist Literature." *Buddhist Annual of Ceylon* (1922).

Wurzburger, Walter S. *Ethics of Responsibility: Pluralistic Approaches to Covenantal Ethics*. Philadelphia, 1994.

Zizek, Slavoj. *Welcome to the Desert of the Real*. London and New York, 2002.

GLOSSARY

adab al-ikhtilaf	Courtesy in academic disputes
al-fana' fi'l-aqida	'Annihilation in doctrine'
asbab	Proximate causes in God's creation
dar al-islam	The 'Abode of Islam', defined by most scholars as all places where Islamic rites are tolerated.
futuwwa	Chivalry
ghuluww	Extremism, excess
jahili	Pertaining to the pagan, pre-Islamic 'Age of Ignorance'
Kharijite	Member of an early extremist-literalist sect.
kufr	Unbelief, 'covering-up' the reality of God.
Uhud	Battle in which the early Muslims were defeated by pagans.